Trump
What He Knows

By Al Newan

Copyright 2017

NOTHING

NOTHING

NOTHING

NOTHING

NOTHING

NOTHING

NOTHING

NOTHING

NOTHING

NOTHING

NOTHING

NOTHING

NOTHING

NOTHING

NOTHING

NOTHING

NOTHING

NOTHING

NOTHING

NOTHING

NOTHING

NOTHING

NOTHING

NOTHING

NOTHING

NOTHING

NOTHING

NOTHING

NOTHING

NOTHING

NOTHING

NOTHING

NOTHING

NOTHING

NOTHING

NOTHING

NOTHING

NOTHING

NOTHING

NOTHING

NOTHING

NOTHING

NOTHING

NOTHING

NOTHING

NOTHING

NOTHING

NOTHING

NOTHING

NOTHING

NOTHING

NOTHING

NOTHING

NOTHING

NOTHING

NOTHING

NOTHING

NOTHING

NOTHING

NOTHING

NOTHING

NOTHING

NOTHING

NOTHING

NOTHING

NOTHING

NOTHING

NOTHING

NOTHING

NOTHING

NOTHING

NOTHING

NOTHING

NOTHING

NOTHING

NOTHING

NOTHING

NOTHING

NOTHING

NOTHING

NOTHING

NOTHING

NOTHING

NOTHING

NOTHING

NOTHING

NOTHING

NOTHING

NOTHING

NOTHING

NOTHING

NOTHING

NOTHING

NOTHING

NOTHING

NOTHING

NOTHING

NOTHING

NOTHING

NOTHING

NOTHING

NOTHING

NOTHING

NOTHING

NOTHING

NOTHING

NOTHING

NOTHING

NOTHING

NOTHING

NOTHING

NOTHING

NOTHING

NOTHING

NOTHING

NOTHING

NOTHING

NOTHING

NOTHING

NOTHING

NOTHING

NOTHING

NOTHING

NOTHING

NOTHING

NOTHING

NOTHING

NOTHING

NOTHING

NOTHING

NOTHING

NOTHING

NOTHING

NOTHING

NOTHING

NOTHING

NOTHING

NOTHING

NOTHING

NOTHING

NOTHING

NOTHING

NOTHING

NOTHING

NOTHING

NOTHING

NOTHING

NOTHING

NOTHING

NOTHING

NOTHING

NOTHING

NOTHING

NOTHING

NOTHING

NOTHING

NOTHING

NOTHING

NOTHING

NOTHING

NOTHING

NOTHING

NOTHING

NOTHING

NOTHING

NOTHING

NOTHING

NOTHING

NOTHING

NOTHING

NOTHING

NOTHING

NOTHING

NOTHING

NOTHING

NOTHING

NOTHING

NOTHING

NOTHING

www.ingramcontent.com/pod-product-compliance
Lightning Source LLC
Chambersburg PA
CBHW071353280526
45787CB00001B/315